THE NEGRO

AND

THE NATION

BY

HUBERT ·H. HARRISON

ISBN: 978-1-63923-818-7

Printed: March 2023

Published and Distributed By:
Lushena Books
607 Country Club Drive, Unit E
Bensenville, IL 60106
www.lushenabks.com

ISBN: 978-1-63923-818-7

PREFACE

This little book is made up of articles contributed several years ago to radical newspapers and magazines like The Call, The Truth-Seeker, Zukunft, and The International Socialist Review. They are re-published in this form, partly to preserve a portion of the author's early work, but mainly because they help to throw into strong relief the present situation of the Negro in present day America, and to show how that situation re-acts upon the mind of the Negro. That is the great need of the Negro at this time.

Some time in the near future I hope to write a little book on the New Negro which will set forth the aims and ideals of the new Manhood Movement among American Negroes which has grown out of the international crusade "for democracy—for the right of those who submit to authority to have A VOICE in their own government"— as President Wilson so sincerely puts it.

Because I wish this little book to have as large a circulation as possible among Negroes and white people, I have preferred publication at a popular price to the doubtful advantage of having a prominent publisher's name at the foot of the title-page. The present edition consists of five thousand copies. When it is sold off a second edition will be issued.

HUBERT H. HARRISON

New York, August, 1917.

THE BLACK MAN'S BURDEN

Providence, according to Mr. Kipling, has been pleased to place upon the white man's shoulders the tremendous burden of regulating the affairs of men of all other colors, who, for the purpose of his argument, are backward and undeveloped—"half devil and half child." When one considers that of the sixteen hundred million people living upon this earth, more than twelve hundred million are colored, this seems a truly staggering burden.

But it does not seem to have occurred to the proponents of this pleasant doctrine that the shoe may be upon the other foot so far as the other twelve hundred million are concerned. It is easy to maintain an **ex parte** argument, and as long as we do not ask the other side to state their case our own arguments will appear not only convincing but conclusive. But in the court of common sense this method is not generally allowed and a case is not considered closed until **both** parties have been heard from.

I have no doubt but that the colored peoples of

NOTE: This article and the next were contributed to the International Socialist Review in 1912 while the author was a member of the Socialist Party. He has since left it (but has joined no other party) partly because, holding as he does by the American doctrine of "Race First," he wished to put himself in a position to work among his people along lines of his own choosing.

the world will have a word or two to say in their own defense. In this article I propose to put the case of the black man in America, not by any elaborate arguments, but by the presentation of certain facts which will probably speak for themselves.

I am not speaking here of the evidences of Negro advancement, nor even making a plea for justice. I wish merely to draw attention to certain pitiful facts. This is all that is necessary—at present. For I believe that those facts will furnish such a damning indictment of the Negro's American over-lord as must open the eyes of the world. The sum total of these facts and of what they suggest constitute a portion of the black man's burden in America. Not all of it, to be sure, but quite enough to make one understand what the Negro problem is. For the sake of clarity I shall arrange them in four groups: political, economic, educational and social.

I—Political.

In a republic all the adult male natives are citizens. If in a given community some are citizens and others subjects, then your community is not a republic. It may call itself so. But that is another matter. Now, the essence of citizenship is the exercise of political rights; the right to a voice in government, to say what shall be done with your taxes, and the right to express your own needs. If you are denied these rights you are not a citizen. Well, in sixteen southern states there are over eight million Negroes in this anomalous position.

4

Of course, many good people contend that they may be unfit to exercise the right of suffrage. If that is so, then who is fit to exercise it for them? This argument covers a fundamental fallacy in our prevailing conception of the function of the ballot. We think that it is a privilege to be conferred for "fitness." But it isn't. It is an instrument by which the people of a community express their will, their wants and their needs. And all those are entitled to use it who have wants, needs and desires that are worth consideration by society. If they are not worth considering, then be brutally frank about it; say so, and establish a protectorate over them. But have done with the silly cant of "fitness." People vote to express their wants. Of course, they will make mistakes. They are not gods. But they have a right to make their own mistakes—the Negroes. All other Americans have. That is why they had Ruef in San Francisco, and still have Murphy in New York.

But the American republic says, in effect, that eight million Americans shall be political serfs. Now, this might be effected with decency by putting it into the national constitution. But it isn't there. The national constitution has two provisions expressly penalizing this very thing. Yet the government—the President, Congress, the Supreme Court—wink at it. This is not what we call political decency. But, just the same, it is done. How is it done? By fraud and force. Tillman of South Carolina has told in the United States

Senate how the ballot was taken from Negroes by shooting them—that is, by murder. But murder is not necessary now. In certain southern states in order to vote a man must have had a grandfather who voted before Negroes were freed. In others, he must be able to interpret and understand any clause in the Constitution, and a white registration official decides whether he does understand. And the colored men of states like Virginia, North Carolina, Georgia, Alabama, Mississsippi and Louisiana who meet such tests as those states provide are disfranchised by the "white primary" system. According to this system only those who vote at the primaries can vote at the general elections. But the South Carolina law provides that: "At this election only white voters. . . and such Negroes as voted the Democratic ticket in 1876 and have voted the Democratic ticket continuously since. . . may vote." Of course, they know that none of them voted that ticket in 1876 or have done so continuously since. In Georgia the law says that: "All white electors who have duly registered . . . irrespective of past political affiliations . . . are hereby declared qualified and are invited to participate in said primary election.

Under the n e w suffrage l a w o f Mr. Booker T. Washington's state of Alabama, Montgomery county, which has 53,000 Negroes, disfranchises all but one hundred of them. In 1908 the Democrats of West Virginia declared in their platform that the United States Constitution should be so amended so as to disfranchise all the

6

Negroes of the country. In December, 1910, the lower house of the Texas legislature, by a vote of 51 to 34, instructed its federal Senators and Congressmen to work for the repeal of the two amendments to the national constitution which confer the right of suffrage upon Negroes. But the funniest proposal in that direction came from Georgia, where J. J. Slade proposed an amendment to the state constitution to the effect that colored men should be allowed to vote only if two **chaste** white women would swear that they would trust them in the dark. But, however it has been effected, whether by force or fraud, by methods wise or otherwise, the great bulk of the Negroes of America are political pariahs to-day. When it is remembered that they once had the right of suffrage, that it was given them, not upon any principle of abstract right, but as a means of protection from the organized ill-will of their white neighbors, that that ill-will is now more effectively organized and in possession of all the powers of the state,—it can be seen at a glance that this spells subjection certain and complete.

II—Economic.

Political rights are the only sure protection and guarantee of economic rights. Every fool knows this. And yet, here in America to-day we have people who tell Negroes that they ought not to agitate for the ballot so long as they still have a chance to get work in the south. And Negro leaders, hired by white capitalists who want cheap labor-power, still continue to mislead both their own and other people. The following facts will demonstrate the economic insecurity of the Negro in the South.

Up to a few years ago systematic peonage was wide-spread in the South. Now, peonage is slavery unsanctioned by law. In its essence it is more degrading than mere chattel slavery. Any one who doubts this may look to modern Mexico for proofs. This peonage in the South had reduced many black men to slavery. And it isn't stamped out yet. It was on January 3, 1911, that the Supreme Court, in the case of Alonzo Bailey, declared unconstitutional the Alabama peonage law, which had been upheld by the state Supreme Bench. About the same time W. S. Harlan, a nephew of the late Justice Harlan of the United States Supreme Court, and manager of a great lumber and turpentine trust, doing business in Florida and Alabama, was sentenced to eighteen months' imprisonment and fined $5,000 for peonage. He has since been pardoned and had his fine remitted by President Taft.

One of the forms of this second slavery is the proprietary system, according to which the Negro laborer or tenant farmer must get his supply at the proprietor's store—and he gets it on credit. The accounts are cooked so that the Negro is always in debt to the modern slave-holder. Some of them spend a life-time working out an original debt of five or ten dollars.

But peonage isn't all. The professional south-

8

erner is always declaring that whatever else the south may not do for the Negro it supplies him with work. It does—when he works for some one else. When he works for himself it is very often different. For instance, there was the Georgia Railroad strike of May, 1909. The Negro firemen were getting from fifty cents to a dollar a day less than the white firemen, they had to do menial work, and could not be promoted to be engineers. They could be promoted, however, to the best runs by the rule of seniority. But the white firemen, who had fixed the economic status of the black firemen, objected to even this. They went on strike and published a ukase to the people of the state in which they said: "The white people of this state refuse to accept social equality."

On the eighth of March, 1911, the firemen of the Cincinnati, New Orleans & Texas Pacific Railroad did the same thing. In the attacks made on the trains by them and their sympathizers many Negro firemen were killed. Occurences of this sort are increasing in frequency and they have a certain tragic significance. It means that the Negro, stripped of the ballot's protection, holds the right to earn his bread at the mere sufferance of the whites. It means that no black man shall hold a job that any white man wants. And that, not in the South alone. There is the case of the Pavers' Union of New York City. The colored pavers, during the panic of 1907, got behind in their dues. The usual period granted expired on Friday. On Monday they sent in their dues in full to the national organization. The treasurer refused to receive the dues and at once got out an injunction against them. This injunction estopped them from appealing to the National Executive Committee or to the national convention. They are still fighting the case.

In January 1911 the several walking delegates of the Painters' Plumbers', Masons,' Carpenters', Steam Fitters', Plasterers' and Tinsmiths' Unions compelled the Thompson & Starrett Construction Co., the second largest firm of contractors in New York, to get rid of the colored cold painters who were engaged on the annex to Stearns' department store. They would not admit them to membership in the union; they merely declared that colored men would not be allowed to do this work. And these are the same men who denounce Negro strik-breakers. They want them out of the unions and also want them to fight for the unions. Presumably they would have them eating air-balls in the meanwhile.

In February 1911 the New York Cab Company was dropping its Negro cab drivers, because, it said, its patrons demanded it. In November 1911 the white chauffeurs of New York were trying to terrorize the colored chauffeurs by a system of sabotage in the garage, because they, too, believed that these jobs were white men's jobs.

It is but a short step from the denial of the right to work to the denial of the right to own. In fact, the two are often linked together, as in the next case. In the latter part of 1910, land speculators in Hominy Okla., sold some land for cotton farms to Negroes. The Negroes paid for this land, took possession, and were getting along splendidly when—"the local whites protested." "Night-riders (i. e., Ku Klux) around Hominy, several days before, served notice that all Negroes must leave the town at once, and to emphasize the warning they exploded dynamite in the neighborhood of Negro houses." So the Negroes fled, fearing for their lives. At Baxterville, Miss., the same thing happened in March 1912. In November 1910, a colored man named Matthew Anderson in Kansas City was having a fine $5,000 house built. But the jealousy of the white neighbors prevented its completion. It was blown up by dynamite when it had been almost finished. In Warrenton, Ga., notice was sent to three colored men and one widow, who had prospered greatly in business, to the effect that they must leave immediately because the white people of Warrenton "were not a-goin' to stand for rich niggers." One of them has been forced to sell out his business at a loss. Another never answers a knock and never leaves his house by the front door. All through these things Mr. Washington told his race that if it would work hard, get property and be useful to a community it would not need to strive for a share in the government!

III—EDUCATIONAL.

EDUCATION is the name which we give to

11

that process of equipment and training which, in our day, society gives the individual to prepare him for fighting the battle of life. We do not confer it as a privilege, but it is given on behalf of society for society's own protection from the perils of ignorance and incompetence. It is a privilege to which every member of society is entitled. For without some equipment of this sort the individual is but half a man, handicapped in the endeavor to make a living. Here in America, we subscribe to the dangerous doctrine that twelve million of the people should receive the minimum of education. And in order to reconcile ourselves to this doctrine, we deck it in the garments of wisdom. Because of the serf idea in American life, we say that the Negro shall have a serf's equipment and no more. It is the same idea that the aristocracy of Europe evolved when the workers demanded that their children should be trained better than they themselves had been. "Why", said the masters, "if we give your children schooling they will be educated out of their station in life. What should the son of a carpenter need to know of Euclid or Virgil? He should learn his father's vocation that he may be well equipped to serve in that station of life into which it has pleased God to call him. We need more plowmen than priests, more servants than savants."

In our own land, when Negroes demand education, we say, "Why, surely, give them industrial education. Your race has a great opportunity—

to make itself useful. It needs trained craftsmen and workers and, perhaps, a few parsons. Teach your sons and daughters to work. That is enough." And we dexterously select leaders for them who will administer the soothing syrup of this old idea with deftness and dispatch. The General Education Board which disburses millions of dollars annually in the South for education has, so far, given to forty-one Negro schools the sum of $464,015. Only in two instances has any money been given to a real college. Practically all of it went to the labor-caste schools. Why? Because the dark degradation of the Negro must be lightened by no ray of learning. That would never do. We need them as "hewers of wood and drawers of water." And in the meanwhile, this is what the richest country on earth offers to ruthlessly exploited people as a training for life:

Before the Twelfth Annual Conference for Education in the South (1910) Mr. Charles L. Coon, superintendent of schools in North Carolina, read a paper on Negro Education in the South. His investigation extended over eleven states: Virginia, North Carolina, South Carolina, Georgia, Florida, Alabama, Mississippi, Louisiana, Texas, Arkansas and Tennessee. In these states the Negroes make up 40.1 per cent of the population, but receive only 14.8 per cent of the school fund. He showed that even if the school fund as disbursed were apportioned to each race according to taxes paid the colored people of Virginia should receive $507,305 instead of the $482,228 which they now receive; in North Carolina they should get $429,127 instead of $402,658, and in Georgia $547,852 instead of $506,-170. So that these three states expend for Negro education $93,278 less than what the Negroes themselves pay for—and that sum is contributed by Negroes to the white children of the state!

But, as a matter of fact, in no modern country is education made to depend upon the tax-paying power of the parents. If that were so, the children of 40,000,000 American proletarians would live and die without schooling. So that the case is really much worse than it seems.

South Carolina spent in 1910 $10.34 for the education of each white child and $1.70 for the education of each colored child. In Lawrence county the state gave to each colored child 97 cents worth of education that year; in Lexington county, 90 cents; in Bamberg, 89 cents; in Saluda, 68 cents, and in Calhoun, 58 cents worth. The smallest sum spent on a white child for education that year was $4.03. In Georgia it was quite as bad. One county of this state owned 19 of the 27 school houses for Negroes. The valuation of the entire 19 was $2,500; that is, $131.58 for each school house for Negroes! The annual cost of the education of a Negro child in six counties of this civilized state was 39 cents. Meanwhile the whites of Baltimore were protesting against the building of a new Negro school! In Louisiana the report of the Department of Education shows that the average monthly salary of white male teachers is 75.29, while that of colored male teachers is $34.25. The average monthly salary of white female teachers is $50.80 and that of the colored female teachers is $28.67. The average length of the annual school term for white children is eight months and a quarter; for colored children, four months and a half.

In Wilcox County, Alabama, where there are 2,000 white children and 10,758 colored children, $32, 660.48 is devoted to education. Of this amount the 10,758 colored children receive one-fourth—$6,-532.09, or sixty cents each per annum—while the 2,000 white children receive the remaining four-fifths—$26,128.13, or about $13 each per annum. Mr. Booker Washington, who lives in this state sends his own children to the best colleges and to Europe while advising the rest of his people to "make your condition known to the white people of the state." Now, if education—of any sort—is a training for life, is it not evident here that black children are being robbed of their chance in life? Why? Is it to be supposed that their fathers are so stupid as to allow this if they could vote their own needs? Yet Mr. Washington decries the agitation for the ballot as unwise and never loses an opportunity of sneering at these who see something of value in it. But to continue. The number of white children of school age in Alabama is 364,266; the number of colored children of school age is 311,552. But the teachers of the white children receive in salaries $2,404,062.54, while the teachers of the colored children receive $202,251.13. The value of all schoolhouses, sites and furniture for white children is $6,503,019.57; for colored children, $273,147.50.

In South Carolina there are 316,007 Negro childen of school age and 201,868 white children; but the state spends on its Negro children $368,802, and on its white children $1,684,976. Thus does America keep knowledge from Negroes. She is afraid of the educated black man. Of such are the people who taunt Negroes with ignorance.

IV.—Social.

When a group has been reduced to serfdom, political and economic, its social status become fixed by that fact. And so we find that in " the home of the free and the land of the brave" Negroes must not ride in the same cars in a train as white people. On street-cars, certain sections are set apart for them. They may not eat in public places where white people eat nor drink at the same bar. They may not go to the same church (although they are foolish enough to worship the same god) as white people; they may not die in the same hospital nor be buried in the same grave-yard. So far as we know, the segregation ends here.

But why is segregation necessary? Because white Americans are afraid that their inherent superiority may not, after all, be so very evident either to the Negro or to other people. They, therefore, find it necessary to enact it into law. So we had the first Ghetto legislation in an American

16

nation last year, in Baltimore. Hard on the heels
of this followed legislative proposals along the
same line in Richmond Va., Kansas City, Mo., St.
Louis, Mo., and Birmingham, Ala. In Memphis,
῾ ..i. ᴦegroes pay taxes for public parks which
they are not allowed to enter. A year ago they
petitioned for a Negro park and were about to get
it when 500 white citizens protested against it.
That settled it with the park.

But discrimination goes even further and declares that Negroes shall not possess even their
lives if any white perons should want them. And
so we have the institution called the lynching-bee.
The professional southerner seems to love a lie
dearly and continues to assert that Negroes are
lynched for rape committed upon white women.
Why not? It is perfectly American. If you want
to kill a dog, call it mad; if you want to silence a
man, call him an Anarchist, and if you want to kill
·a black man, call him a rapist. But let us see what
the facts actually are.

In the two decades from 1884 to 1904 there
were 2,875 lynchings in the United States. Of
these 87 per cent, or 2,499 occurred in the South.
The national total was grouped as follows:

1. For alleged and attempted criminal assault,
   i. e., rape 564
2. For assault and murder and for complicity 138
3. For murder 1,277
4. For theft, burglary and robbery 326
5. For arson 106

17

The causes for the remainder wer: slander, miscegenation, informing, drunkenness, fraud, voodooism, violation of contract, resisting arrest, elopement, train wrecking, poisoning stock, refusing to give evidence, testifying against whites, political animosity, disobedience of quarantine regulations, passing counterfeit money, introducing smallpox, concealing criminals, cutting levees, kidnapping, gambling, riots, seduction, incest, and forcing a child to steal.

Yes, there are courts in the South; but not for black people—n o t w h e n t h e m o b chooses to relieve civilization of the onus of law and order. At Honeapath, S. C., a Negro was lynched in November 1911, charged, of course, with "the usual crime." The charge had not been proven, or invetsigated; but the man was lynched. The howling mob which did him to death was composed of "prominent citizens" who had made up automobile parties to ride to the affair. Among those present was the dis-honorable Joshua Ashley, a member of the state legislature. He and his friends cut off the man's fingers as souvenirs and were proud of their work. Why shouldn't they? You see, it helps to keep "niggers" in their place. And then, besides, isn't this a white man's country?

Gov. Blease of South Carolina was also proud of the event and said that instead of stopping the horrible work of the mob he would have resigned his office to lead it. In Okemeah, Oklahoma, last June, a band of white beasts raped a Negro woman and then lynched her and her fourteen-year-old son. Nothing has been done to them. And it is not that the facts are unknown. At Durant, Okla., and elsewhere, the savages have posed around their victim to have their pictures taken. One man, from Alabama, sent to the Rev. John Haynes Holmes, of Brooklyn, N. Y., a post-card (by mail) bearing a photograph of such a group. "This is the way we treat them down here," he writes, and, after promising to put Mr. Holmes' name on his mailing list, declares that they will have one, at least, each month.

In Washington, Ga., Charles S. Holinshead, a wealthy white planter, raped the wife of T. B. Walker, a decent. respectable Negro. As his wife returned to him dishevelled and bleeding from the outrage perpetrated on her, Walker went to Holinshead's store and shot him dead. For this he was tried and condemned and, while the judge was yet pronouncing sentence, Holinshead's brother shot Walker in the court-room. They held his head up while the judge finished the sentence. Then he was taken out and lynched—not executed. Nothing was done to the other Holinshead.

The New York Evening Post, on Octoer 23rd, said in an editorial that "there has hardly been a single authenticated case in a decade of the Negroes rising against the whites, despite the growing feeling, among them that there should be some retaliation since no tribunal will punish lynchers or enforce the law." I am glad that the **Post** noticed this. I had begun to notice it myself. When President Roosevelt discussed lynching some years ago, he severely reprobated **the Negro** for their tendency to shield their "criminals" and ordered them to go out and help hunt them down. So was insult added to injury.

But, putting my own opinion aside, here are the facts as I have seen them. In the face of these facts, the phrase, "the white man's burden," souı.ds like a horrid mockery.

——: o :——

SOCIALISM AND THE NEGRO

1. Economic Status Of The Negro

The ten million Negroes of America form a group that is more essentially proletarian than any other American group. In the first place the ancestors of this group were brought here with the very definite understanding that they were to be ruthlessly exploited. And they were not allowed any choice in the matter. Since they were brought here as chattels their social status was fixed by that fact. In every case that we know of where a group has lived by exploiting another group, it has despised that group which it has put under subjection. And the degree of contempt has always been in direct proportion to the degree of exploitation·

Inasmuch then, as the Negro was at one period the most thoroughly exploited of the American proletariat, he was the most thoroughly despised. That group which exploited and despised him, being the most powerful section of the ruling class, was able to diffuse its own necessary contempt of the Negro first among the other sections of the ruling class, and afterwards among all other classes of Americans. For the ruling class has always determined what the social ideals and moral ideas of society should be; and this explains how race prejudice was disseminated until all Americans are supposed to be saturated with it. Race prejudice, then, is the fruit of economic subjection and a fixed inferior economic status. It is the reflex of a so-cial caste system. That caste system in America today is what we roughly refer to as the Race Problem, and it is thus seen that the Negro prob-lem is essentialliy an economic problem with its roots in slavery past and present.

Notwithstanding the fact that it is usually kept out of public discussion, the bread-and-butter side of this problem is easily the most important. The Negro worker gets less for his work—thanks to exclusion from the craft unions—than any other worker; he works longer hours as a rule and under worse conditions than any other worker, and his rent in any large city is much higher than that which the white worker pays for the same tene-ment. In short, the exploitation of the Negro worker is keener than that of any group of white workers in America. Now, the mission of the So-cialist Party is to free the working class from ex-ploitation, and since the Negro is the most ruth-lessly exploited working class group in America, the duty of the party to champion his cause is as clear as day. This is the crucial test of Socialism's sincerity and therein lies the value of this point of view—Socialism and the Negro·

2. The Need of Socialist Propaganda.

So far, no particular effort has been made to carry the message of Socialism to these people. All the rest of the poor have had the gospel preach-ed to them, for the party has carried on special propaganda work among the Poles, Slovaks, Finns, Hungarians and Lithuanians. Here are ten million Americans, all proletarians, hanging on the ragged edge of the impending class conflict. Left to themselves they may become as great a menace to our advancing army as is the army of the unemployed, and for precisely the same reason: they can be used against us, as the craft unions have begun to find out· Surely we should make some effort to enlist them under our banner that they may swell our ranks and help to make us invincible. And we must do this for the same reason that is impelling organized labor to adopt an all-inclusive policy; because the other policy results in the artificial breeding of scabs. On grounds of common sense and enlightened self-interest it would be well for the Socialist party to begin to organize the Negroes of America in reference to the class struggle· The capitalists of America are not waiting. Already they have subsidized Negro leaders, Negro editors, preachers and politicians to build up in the breasts of the black people those sentiments which will make them subservient to their will. For they recognize the value (to them) of cheap labor power and they know that if they can succeed in keeping one section of the working class down they can use that section to keep other sections down too.

3. The Negro's Attitude Toward Socialism.

If the Socialist propaganda among Negroes is be effectively carried on, the members and leaders of the party must first understand the Negro's attitude toward Socialism· That attitude finds its first expression in ignorance. The mass of the Negro people in America are ignorant of what Socialism means. For this they are not much to blame· Behind the veil of the color line none of the great world-movements for social betterment have been able to penetrate. Since it is not yet the easiest task to get the white American worker—with all his superior intellect—to see Socialism, it is but natural to expect that these darker workers to whom America denies knowledge should still be in ignorance as to its aims and objects.

Besides, the Negroes of America—those of them who think—are suspicious of Socialism as of everything that comes from the white people of America. They have seen that every movement for the extension of democracy here has broken down as soon as it reached the color line. Political democracy declared that "all men are created equal," meant only all white men. The Christian church found that the brotherhood of man did not include God's bastard children. The public school system proclaimed that the school house was the backbone of democracy—"for white people only," and the civil service says that Negroes must keep their place—at the bottom. So that they can hardly be blamed for looking askance at any new gospel of freedom· Freedom to them has been like one of "those juggling fiends.

SOCIALISM AND THE NEGRO

That palter with us in a double sense;
That keep the word of promise to our ear,
And break it to our hope."

In this connection, some explanation of the former political solidarity of those Negroes who were voters may be of service· Up to six years ago the one great obstacle to the political progress of the colored people was their sheep-like allegiance to the Republican party. They were taught to believe that God had raised up a peculiar race of men called Republicans who had loved the slaves so tenderly that they had taken guns in their hands and rushed on the ranks of the southern slaveholders to free the slaves; that this race of men was still in existence, marching under the banner of the Republican party and showing their great love for Negroes by appointing from six to sixteen near-Negroes to soft political snaps. Today that great political superstition is falling to pieces before the advance of intelligence among Negroes. They begin to realize that they were sold out by the Republican party in 1876; that in the last twenty-five years lynchings have increased, disfranchisement has spread all over the south and "jim-crow" cars run even into the national capital —with the continuing consent of a Republican congress, a Republican Supreme Court and Republican presidents.

Ever since the Brownsville affair, but more clearly since Taft declared and put in force the policy of pushing out the few near-Negro officeholders, the rank and file have come to see that the Republican party is a great big sham. Many went over to the Democratic party because, as the Amsterdam News puts it, "they had nowhere else to go." Twenty years ago the colored men who joined that party were ostracized as scalawags and crooks—which they probably were. But today, the defection to the Democrats of such men as Bishop Walters, Wood, Carr and Langston—whose uncle was a colored Republican congressman from Virginia—has made the colored democracy respectable and given quite a tone to political heterodoxy·

All this loosens the bonds of their allegiance and breaks the bigotry of the last forty years. But of this change in their political view-point the white world knows nothing· The two leading Negro newspapers are subsidized by the same political pirates who held the title-deeds to the handful of hirelings holding office in the name of the Negro race. One of these papers is an organ of Mr. Washington, the other pretends to be independent—that is, it must be "bought" on the installment plan, and both of them are in New York. Despite this "conspiracy of silence" the Negroes are waking up; are beginning to think for themselves; to look with more favor on "new doctrines." And herein lies the open opportunity of the Socialist party. If the work of spreading Socialist propaganda is taken to them now, their ignorance of it can be enlightened and their suspicions removed.

SOCIALISM AND THE NEGRO

The Duty of The Socialist Party.

I think that we might embrace the opportunity of taking the matter up at the coming national convention· The time is ripe for taking a stand against the extensive disfranchisement of the Negro in violation of the plain provisions óf the national constitution. In view of the fact that the last three amendments to the constitution contain the clause, "Congress shall have power to enforce this article by appropriate legislation," the party will not be guilty of proposing anything worse than asking the government to enforce its own "law and order." If the Negroes, or any other section of the working class in America, is to be deprived of the ballot, how can they participate with us in the class struggle? How can we pretend to be a political party if we fail to see the significance of this fact?

Besides, the recent dirty diatribes against the Negro in a Texas paper, which is still on our national list of Socialist papers; the experiences of Mrs. Theresa Malkiel in Tennessee where she was prevented by certain people from addressing a meeting of Negroes on the subject of Socialism, and certain other exhibitions of the thing called southernism, constitute the challenge of caste. Can we ignore this challenge? I think not. We could hardly afford to have the taint of "trimming" on the garments of the Socialist party. It is dangerous—doubly dangerous now, when the temper of the times is against such "trimming." Besides it would be futile. If it is not met now it must be met later when it shall have grown stronger. Now, when we can cope with it, we have the issue squarly presented: Southernism or Socialism—which? Is it to be the white half of the working class against the black half, or all the working class? Can we hope to triumph over capitalism with one-half of the working class against us? Let us settle these questions now—for settled they must be.

The Negro and Political Socialism.

ꞁ The power of the voting proletariat can be made to express itself through the ballot· To do this they must have a political organization of their own to give form to their will. The direct object of such an organization is to help them to secure control of the powers of government by electing members of the working class to office and so secure legislation in the interests of the working class until such time as the workers may, by being in overwhelming control of the government, be able "to alter or abolish it, and to institute a new government, laying its foundation on such principles, and organizing its power in such form, as to them shall seem most likely to effect their safety and happiness"—in short, to work for the abolition of capitalism, by legislation—if that be permitted. And in all this, the Negro, who feels most fiercely the deep damnation of the capitalist system, can help·

The Negro and Industrial Socialism.

But even the voteless proletarian can in a

28

measure help toward the final abolition of the capitalist system. For they too have labor power—which they can be taught to withhold. They can do this by organizing themselves at the point of production. By means of such organization they can work to shorten the hours of labor, to raise wages, to secure an ever-increasing share of the product of their toil. They can enact and enforce laws for the protection of labor and they can do this at the point of production, as was done by the Western Federation of Miners in the matter of the eight-hour law, which they established without the aid of the legislatures or the courts. All this involves a progressive control of the tools of production and a progressive expropriation of the capitalist class. And in all this the Negro can help· So far, they are unorganized on the industrial field, but industrial unionism beckons to them as to others, and the consequent program of the Socialist party for the Negro in the south can be based upon this fact.

————:o:————

THE REAL NEGRO PROBLEM

The African slave-trade was born of the desire of certain Europeans to acquire wealth without working. It was to fill the need for a cheap labor supply in developing new territory that Negro slaves were first brought to the western world by the Spanish, Dutch, and English during the 16th and 17th centuries. Contact of white with black was thus established on the basis of the economic subjection of the one to the other. This subjection extended to every sphere of life, physical, mental and social. Out of this contact there arose certain definite relations and consequent problems of adjustment. It is the sum of these relations which we (rightly or wrongly) describe as the Negro Problem.

Unfortunately, the spell of mere words is still very strong, and when people speak of the Negro Problem they carry over into the discussion a certain mental attitude derived from the original meaning of the word, Problem. In arithmetic, a sum to be worked out; in chemistry, to find by experiment a certain re-agent; in geography, to chart a puzzling current—all these are problems in the primary sense, and all these involve the idea of solution by him who approaches them. That is to say, they can be solved **by thinking.** And those who think loosely call up this idea of solution by thinking whenever they see the word "problem". So we have been pestered with this, that, and the other "solution" of the Negro problem. Therefore, it is well to bear in mind that a race problem is always the sum of the relations between two or more races in a state of friction.

Because when we understand this we are in a fair way to find that these relations are not to be explained on the basis of the thinking or feeling of either party. They must be interpreted in terms of human relations and in the order in which human relations are established: (1) economic, (2) social, (3) political and (4) civic. So understood, a knowledge of the historical conditions under which these relations developed is seen to be of the greatest value in understanding the problem. For this is all that our intellects can do in the case of a racial problem—to help us to understand. The actual work of adjustment must be fought out or worked out; becomes, that is to say, a struggle to be set-tled by the contending races with forces more complex than the purely intellectual ones of argument and proof. Let us first consider, then, the conditions under which the relations between the black and white races were established in America·

During the period of colonization the land of America was granted by European kings to certain gentlemen who had no intention of working with the hands. Nevertheless working with the hands was the only method of extracting that wealth which was the object of their ownership. it was necessary, then, to obtain a supply of those persons who could do this work for them; and to

31

insure this, it was imperative that these persons should not own land themselves: they must be a permanently landless class; since it was unthinkable then as now that one should work the land of others for a part of the fruits if he could work his own land for all of the fruits· So there was begun in America the process of establishing such a class. Confining ourselves to the territory which became the United States, we may say that the first attempt was made to enslave the Indians, and when this failed to work, white people were imported from Europe as chattel slaves. All through the colonial period this importation continued with its consequent effects on the social and political life of the colonies. Most people will be surprised to learn that the first Fugitive Slave Law was framed, not in the south, but in the north, and was made not for black but for white laborers. This was the Massachusetts act of 1630 "Respecting Masters, Servants and Laborers". A reading of this one act would destroy all those pretty illusions about "our fathers and Freedom" which we get from the official fairy tales—I mean the school histories.

Side by side with the economic subjection of white men there grew up the economic subjection of black men, and for the same reason. These were of alien blood—and cheaper. Therefore, the African slave trade outgrew the European slave trade, although the latter continued, in a lessening degree, down to the third or fourth decade of the

19th century· Negroes were brought here to work, to be exploited; and they were allowed no illusions as to the reason for their being here. Those white men who owned the land brought them here to extract the wealth which was in the land. The white aristocrat did not buy black slaves because he had a special hatred or contempt for anything black, nor because he believed that Negroes were inferior to white people· On the contrary he bought them precisely because, as working cattle, they were superior to whites.

Being of alien blood, these black people were **outside** of the social and political system to which they were introduced and, quite naturally, beyond the range of such sympathies as helped to soften the hard brutalities of the system. They were, from the beginning, more ruthlessly exploited than the white workers. Thus they had their place made for them—at the bottom.

Now it is a social law—not yet proclaimed by our college sociologists—that whenever a certain social arrangement is beneficial to any class in a society, that class soon develops the pyschology of its own advantage and creates insensibly the ethics which will justify that social arrangement. Men to whom the vicarious labor of slaves meant culture and refinement, wealth, leisure and education, naturally came—without any self-deception, to see that slavery was **right.** As Professor Loria points out, there is an economic basis to moral transformations in any society which is built on vicarious production·

We turn now to the resulting conditions of the slaves. They were at the bottom, the most brutally exploited and, therefore, the most despised section of the laboring class. For it is a consequent of the law stated above that those who are exploited must needs be despised by those who exploit them· This mental attitude of the superior class (which makes the laws of that society in which it is dominant) will naturally find its expression in those actions by which they esablish their relations to the inferior class. And whenever anyone is to be kicked it is usually the man farthest down who gets it, because he is most contiguous to the foot. So the Negro having been given a place at the bottom in the economic life of the nation, came to occupy naturally the place at the bottom in the nation's thinking. I say, the nation's advisedly; because the dominant ideas of any society which is already divided into classes are as a rule the ideas preservative of the existing arrangements. But since those arrangements include a class on top, the dominant ideas will generally coincide with the interest of that class. The ethics of its own advantage, then, will be diffused by that class throughout that society—will be, if need arise imposed upon the other classes, since every ruling class has always controlled the public instruments for the diffusion of ideas.

In this way the slave-holding section of the dominant class in America first diffused its own

THE REAL NEGRO PROBLEM

necessary contempt for the Negro among the other
sections of the ruling class, and the ideas of this
class as a whole became through the agency of
press, pulpit and platform, the ideas of "the American People" on the Negro·

In further application of the materialistic
methed to this subject, it is curious and interesting
to note how the southern attitude toward the Negro
changed with the changing industrial system.
When the wasteful agricultural methods of chattel
slavery had exhausted the soil of the south and no
new land loomed up on the horizon of the system,
slavery began to decay. The planters of that section
settled down into the patriarchal type of family
relations with their slaves, who were then simply
a means of keeping the master's hands free from
the contamination of work and not a means of
ever-increasing profits· Slavery was then in a fair
way to die of its own weight. But with the inven-
tion of Whitney's cotton-gin, which enabled one
man to do the work of three hundred, cotton came
to the front as the chief agricultural staple in
America. The black slave became a source of increasing revenue as a fertilizer of capital. The
idyllic relations of the preceding forty years came
to a sudden end. Increased profits demanded increased exploitation and the ethics of advantage
dictated the despising of the Negro.

De Bow's Review, the great organ of southern
opinion, appeared, and in serious scientific articles
maintained the proposition that the Negro was not

a man but a beast. About that time (and conformably to that opinion) the practice was begun of spelling the word, Negro, with a small "n"—a practice still current in America, even in the socialist press.

In the meanwhile, the system of industrial production known as the machine system developed in the north·The factory proletariat whose condition determined that of the other northern workers could fertilize capital more rapidly and cheaply than the slaves. This form of production (and its products) came into competition with the slave system and the tremendous conflict reflected itself upon the political field as a struggle for the restriction of slavery within its original bounds. The Louisiana Purchase, the annexation of Texas, the Missouri Compromise, the Dred Scot Decision, the Kansas-Nebraska Bill,—all these were political episodes in the competition between the two main sections of the dominant class; and in the conflict each used the army, the navy, the executive, the courts and the legislature to strengthen its own position·

When the business interests of the north had definitely captured the powers of government in the general election of 1860, the southerners seceeded because they knew too well what governmental power was generally used for. They wanted a government which would be the political reflex of their own economic dominance. One can see now why the northern statesmen like Lincoln insisted that the preservation of the Union was the paramount issue and not the freedom of slaves. Indeed, Lincoln punished those officers of the army who in the early days of the war dared to act upon that assumption. And not all the arguments of Greeley, Conway and Governor Andrews could make any change in his attitude. Not until he saw that it was expedient "as a war measure" did he issue the "Emancipation Proclamation" which brought 187,000 Negro soldiers into the northern army.

Emancipation gave to the Negroes a new economic status—the status of free wage-laborers, competing with other wage-laborers for work. They who had worked to create wealth for others were now turned loose without wealth or land to shift for themeselves in a world already hostile to them· The mental attitude of the white south had been shaped by three centuries of slavery and was hard to get rid of. It was difficult for them to think of black labor under any form but that of slavery and they naturally turned to compulsion as the proper mode of obtaining work from their former slaves. This attitude was well expressed in the Black Codes of the southern states during the fall and winter of 1865-66. As soon as the end of the hostilities gave them a free hand at home they began to give legislative expression to the new conditions. They framed new constitutions and new laws. "But it was seen that the Negro had no privilege of voting in the first instance, and it was not to be expected that the right would be accorded him under the new state constitutions; no guarantee that justice should be done him was exacted. These new constitutions were formed, the legislatures met, laws were made, senators and representatives to Congress were chosen; but the Negro was not only not admitted to any participation in the government, but the new legislatures shocked the northern sence of justice by the cruel and revengeful laws which they enacted. The barbarity of the most odious slave-code was, under various disguises, applied to the Negro in his new condition of freedom". Even before the resentment of the national legislature had taken form, the Ku-Klux Klan, the Knights of the White Camelias, the Society of the Pale Faces, and other bands of organized representatives of culture had begun to do their bloody work of terrorizing Negroes into economic and social subjection. And all this before any steps had been taken to extend the suffrage to Negroes.

When the northerners investigated these conditions they met with such fierce and unreasoning hostility on the part of the south that they found it necessary to arm the Negro with the ballot in his own defense· And yet, professional southerners like Tom Dixon, Tom Watson, Ben Tillman Vardaman and Blease pretend to their ignorant or forgetful countrymen that the present attitude of the south was caused in the first instance by a reaction against "Negro domination", social and political which the north had forced upon it.

The subsequent developments can not be explained by those amiable enthusiasts who see in the "freedom" of Negroes an act of genuine humanitarianism on the part of the north. For, after the northern business-men had secured the government—and their thousands of miles of railroad-grants—they promptly dropped the mask of humanitarian hypocrisy, and left the Negroes to shift for themselves· During the disputed count of the votes in the Hayes-Tilden electoral contest in 1877 a deal was arranged by which the northerners agreed to withdraw the army which protected the Negroes, newly-granted franchise in the south, on condition that the southerners should concede the election to Hayes. The new industrial order wanted above all things to retain control of the government which it had captured during the war, and upon the altar of this necessity it sacrificed the Negro in the south, just as Lincoln had done in the early days of the war. From that time the suppression of the Negro vote, the growth of "Jim Crow" legislation, lynching and segregation have continued with the continuing consent of Republican congressman, presidents and supreme courts. And through it all, Negro "leaders" like Mr. Washington have found it very much worth their while to administer anodynes both to the Negro and the Nation, to reconcile the one to a bastard democracy and the other to a mutilated manhood.

It would be well to trace here the nature of

the economic changes which have given certain
new and malignant features to the relations between black and white in Amercia. The effect upon the free laborers of the sudden influx of black
competitors in the labor-market; the consequent
attitude of the labor-unions; the political and social reflex of all this, with the vestiges of the old,
re-developing under the new conditions—all these
are parts of the problem. But space will not permit,
and these considerations will be taken up in a second paper. Yet I may indicate here the gist of my
conclusions by quoting the words of a well-known
Southerner, the Rev. Quincy Ewing· "The race
problem—is not that the Negro is what he is in
relation to the white man—the white man's inferior—but this, rather: How to keep him what he is
in relation to the white man; how to prevent his
ever achieving or becoming that which would justify the belief on his part, or on the part of other
people, that he and the white man stand on common human ground."

The economic necessities of a system of vicarious production led to the creation of a racial
labor-caste; the social adjustment consequent upon
this and upon its development created a social
sentiment inimical to this class, and its continuance
requires a continuance of this sentiment in our society; this is the pivotal fact. And the unavoid-
able conclusion is, that when this system of vicarious production disappears, the problem which is
its consequence will disappear also—and not till
then, in spite of all the culture, individual or col-
lective, which that class may achieve.

ON A CERTAIN
CONSERVATISM IN NEGROES

It would be a difficult task to name one line of intellectual endeavor among white men in America, in which the American Negro has not taken his part. Yet it is a striking fact that the racial attitude has been dominantly conservative. Radicalism does not yet register to any noticeable extent the contributions of our race in this country. In theological criticism, religious dissent, social and political heresies such as Single Tax, Socialism, Anarchism —in most of the movements arising from the reconstruction made necessary by the great body of that new knowledge which the last two centuries gave us—the Negro in America has taken no part. And today our sociologists and economists still restrict themselves to the compilation of tables of statistics in proof of Negro progress. Our scholars are still expressing the intellectual viewpoints of the eighteenth century. The glimmer of a change is perceptible only in some of the younger men like Locke of Howard University and James C. Waters, Jr.

It is easy to account for this. Christian America created the color line; and all the great currents of critical opinion, from the eighteenth century to our time, have found the great barrier impassible and well-nigh impervious. Behind the color line one has to think perpetually of the color line, and most of those who grow up behind it can think of nothing else. Even when one essays to think of other things, that thinking is tinged with the shades of the surrounding atmosphere.

Besides, when we consider what Negro education is to-day when we remember that in certain southern counties the munificent sum of 58 cents is spent for the annual education of a Negro child; that the "great leader" of his race decries "higher" education for them; that Negro boys who get as far as "college" must first surmount tremendous special obstacles—we will cease to wonder at the dearth of thinkers who are radical on other than racial matters.

Yet, it should seem that Negroes, of all Americans, would be found in the Freethought fold, since they have suffered more than any other class of Americans from the dubious blessings of Christianity. It has been well said that the two great instruments for the propagation of race prejudice in America are the Associated Press and the Christian Church. This is quite true. Historically, it was the name of religion that cloaked the beginnings of slavery on the soil of America, and buttressed its continuance. The church saw to it that the religion taught to slaves should stress the servile virtues of subservience and content, and these things have bitten deeply into the souls of black folk. True, the treasured music of these darker millions preserves, here and there, the note of stifled rebellion; but this was in spite of religion—not because of it. Besides, such of their "sorrow-songs" as have this note in them were brutally banned by their masters, and driven to the purlieus of the plantation, there to be sung in secret,

CONSERVATISM IN NEGROES

And all through the dark days of slavery, it was
the Bible that constituted the divine sanction of
this "peculiar institution." "Cursed be Canaan,"
"Servants obey your masters" and similar texts
were the best that the slaveholders'‑ Bible could
give of consolation to the brothers in black, while,
for the rest, teaching them to read was made a
crime so that whatever of social dynamite there
might be in certain parts of the book, might not
come near their minds.

Lowell, in his "Biglow Papers," has given a
caustic but correct summary of the Christian slaveholders' theology in regard to the slavery of black
working-people:

"All things wuz gin to man for's use, his sarvice an' de-
　　ht.
An' don't the Greek an' Hebrew words that mean a man
　　mean white?
Ain't it belittlin' the good book in all its proudes' features
To think 't wuz wrote for black an' brown an' 'lasses-col-
　　ored creatures,
Thet couldn' read it ef they would—nor ain't by lor allowed
　　to,
But ought to take wut we think suits their naturs, an' be
　　proud to?
　　*　　　*　　　*　　　*
Where'd their soles go ter, I'd like to know, ef we should
　　let 'em ketch
Freeknowledgism an' Fourierism an' Speritoolism an'
　　sech?"

When the fight for the abolition of slavery was
on, the Christian church, not content with quoting scripture, gagged the mouths of such of their
adherents as dared to protest against the accursed

thing, penalized their open advocacy of abolition, and opposed all the men like Garrison, Lovejoy, Phillips and John Brown, who fought on behalf of the Negro slave. The detailed instances and proofs are given in the last chapter of "A Short History of the Inquisition," wherein the work shows the relation of the church and slavery.

Yet the church among the Negroes today exerts a more powerful influence than anything else in the sphere of ideas. Nietzsche's contention that the ethics of Christianity are the slave's ethics would seem to be justified in this instance. Show me a population that is deeply religious, and I will show you a servile population, content with whips and chains, contumely and the gibbet, content to eat the bread of sorrow and drink the waters of affliction.

The present condition of the Negroes of America is a touching bit of testimony to the truth of this assertion. Here in America the spirit of the Negro has been transformed by three centuries of subjection, physical and mental, so that they have even glorified the fact of subjection and subservience. How many Negro speakers have I not heard vaunting the fact that when in the dark days of the South the Northern armies had the Southern aristocracy by the throat, there was no Negro uprising to make their masters pay for the systematic raping of Negro women and the inhuman cruelties perpetrated on Negro men. And yet the sole reason for this "forbearance" is to be found in the fact that their spirits had been completely crushed by the system of slavery. And to accomplish this, Christianity—the Christianity of their masters—was the most effective instrument.

A recent writer, Mr. E. B. Putnam-Weale, in his book, "The Conflict of Color," has quite naively disclosed the fact that white people are well aware of this aspect of Christianity and use it for their own ends. Mr. Putnam-Weale makes no pretense of believing in the Christian myth himself, but he wants it taught to the Negroes; and comparing it with Islam, he finds it a more efficient instrument of racial subjugation. The Mohammedan, he finds, preaches the equality of all true believers—and lives up to it. The white Christian preaches the brotherhood of man, but wants "niggers" to sit in the rear pews, to ride in "Jim Crow" cars, and generally to "keep in their place." He presents this aspect of the case under the caption of "The Black Samson and the White Delilah," and, with less fear than an angel, frankly advises the white Lords of Empire not so much to civilize as to christianize Africa, so that Deliah's work may be well done.

Here in America her work has been well done; and I fear that many years must pass before the leaders of thought among my people in this country contribute many representatives to the cause o⁻ Freethought. Just now, there are a few Negro Agnostics in New York and Boston, but these are generally found to be West Indians from the

CONSERVATISM IN NEGROES

French, Spanish, and English islands. The Cuban and Porto Rican cigar-makers are notorious Infidels, due to their acquaintance with the bigotry, ignorance and immorality of the Catholic priesthood in their native islands. Here and there one finds a Negro-American who is reputed to have Agnostic tendencies; but these are seldom, if ever, openly avowed. I can hardly find it in my heart to blame them, for I know the tremendous weight of the social proscription which it is possible to bring to bear upon those who dare defy the idols of our tribe. For those who live by the people must needs be careful of the people's gods; and

"An up-to-date statesmen has to be on his guard,

If he must have beliefs not to b'lieve 'em too hard."

Myself, I am inclined to believe that freedom of thought must come from freedom of circumstance; and so long as our "leaders" are dependent on the favor of our masses for their livelihood, just so long will they express the thought of the masses, which of itself may be a good thing or a bad according to the circumstances of the particular case Still there is a terrible truth in Kipling's modern version of Job's sarcastic bit of criticism:

"No doubt but ye are the people—your throne is above the
    King's,
Whoso speaks in your presence must say acceptable
    things;
Bowing the head in worship, bending the knee in fear—
Bringing the word well-smoothen—such as a King should
    hear."

And until this rising generation of Negroes can shake off the trammels of such time-serving leaders as Mr. Washington, and attain the level of that "higher education" against which he solidly sets his face; until they, too, shall have entered into the intellectual heritage of the last two hundred years, there can be little hope of a change in this respect.

———— : o : ————

WHAT SOCIALISM MEANS TO US

In the good old days "when cotton was king", chattel-slavery was a flourishing institution. Not only the people who profited by the system, but most others—even those who were the sufferers—thought that this was really a "law of nature", that it couldn't be otherwise. Nevertheless, chattel slavery has gone. But while it lasted this was its essence: Certain human beings were compelled to labor and the wealth which their labor produced went, not to them, but to certain other human beings who did not labor at all but lolled in luxury on the labor of their slaves.

To-day, fellow-sufferers, they tell us that we are free. But are we? If you will think for a moment you will see that we are not free at all. We have simply changed one form of slavery for another. Then it was chattel-slavery, now it is wage-slavery. For that which was the essence of chattel-slavery is the essence of wage slavery. It is only a difference in form. The chattel-slave was compelled to work by physical force; the wage-slave is compelled to work by starvation. The product of the chattel-slave's labor was taken by his master; the product of the wage-slave's labor is taken by the employer.

The United States Government has made a study of the wealth producing power of the wage-slaves, and has shown that the average worker **produces** $2,451 a year. The government has also made a study of wages in the U. S. which shows that the average worker gets $437 a year. This means that the average employer takes away from the average wage-slave $2,014 a year. In the good old days the master took away the wealth produced by the slave in the simplest form; today he takes it away in the form of profits. But in one respect the wage-slave is worse off than the chattel slave. Under chattel slavery the master owned the man and the land; he had to feed and clothe the man. Under wage-slavery the man feeds and clothes himself. Under chattel slavery it was to the interest of the owner to give the slave work and to keep him from starving to death. Under wage-slavery, if the man goes out of work the employer doesn't care; that is no loss to him; and if the man dies there are millions of others eager to take his place, because, as I said before, they must either work for him or starve. There is one very striking parallel between the two cases. To-day there are many people who say that this system is divinely appointed—is a law of nature —just as they said the same thing of chattel slavery. Well, there are millions of workers who say that it is wrong. Under chattle-slavery black workers were robbed; under wage-slavery all the workers are robbed. The Socialist Party says that this robbing shall cease; that no worker black or white shall be exploited for profit. And it says, further, that there is one sure and certain way of putting an end to the system and that is by working for the success of Socialism.

But, before I tell you just how Socialism proposes to do this, let me say a word about the Civil

War which put an end to chattel-slavery. Now, I know that certain people have taught you to believe that the Civil War was fought to free the slaves. But it isn't true, at all, and only very ignorant people hold that opinion nowadays. If you will read the Emancipation Proclamation carefully you will see that it wasn't for love of the slave that the slaves were freed. You will see that this was done, **"as a fit and neccesary war-measure for suppress-ing said rebellion."** If you will read Lincoln's letter to Horrace Greeley (August 22 nd 1862) you will find this sentence: My paramount object in this struggle is to save the Union and is not either to save or destroy slavery." Now I will tell you briefly how "this struggle" came about. I konw that my explanation is not the one which you have been taught. But, no matter; it happens to be true. This was the way of it: In the South there had grown up one system of exploiting the laborer. That was chattel-slavery. The money-Kings of that section whom we will call capitalists, for short, were naturally fond of their own system. In the North the capitalists had another system of which they were equally fond. That was wage-slavery. The Southern capitalists found that it was necessary to extend their system; so we had the Mexican War, and they got Texas. Then, as fast as new territory was opened they would rush to occupy it with their system and so shut out the Northern system. Of course, the Northern capitalists would try to get their system into the new territory also; so we had the long struggle over Kansas and Ne-

braska. These two systems were then in open
competition and it came to be seen that one or the
other had to give in; that both of them couldn't
exist in the same country; that "a house divided
against itself cannot stand"; that "this nation cannot exist half-slave and half-free." Then people
began to talk of "the impending crisis"; of "the ir-
repressible conflict." Then, when Lincoln was
elected in 1859, the southern capitalists saw that
their system was doomed. They wished to preserve it; so they seceded and tried to make of
themselves a separate nation in which their system
of robbing the worker shold be the only one. But
the Northern capitalists said, "Nix! Our system
shall be the only system." So they went to war
"to save the Union"—for their system of robbing
the workers. And that's the gist of the whole
story.

    "But", you will say, "didn't they go to war
on account of John Brown and Wendell Phillips
and William Lloyd Garrison and Charles Sumner?"
Not on your life, they didn't. If you will read the
newspapers of that time you will see that they
tried to lynch Garrison in Boston; they ostracized
Wendell Phillips; they sneered at Sumner and
damned John Brown. Why, nice, good, Christian
people told them they were crazy—just as some of
them tell Socialists now—and the anti-slavery or-
ators couldn't get the use of a church in New York
either for love or for money. No, indeed. These
men were grand old heroes—but no war was fought

on their account. The older system of chattle-slavery simply broke down to make way for the present system of wage-slavery, which pays better. Pays the capitalist, I mean.

Under the old system the capitalist owned the man; today he own the tools with which the man must work. These tools are the factories, the mines, and the machines. The system that owns them owns you and me and all the rest of us, black, white, brown, red, and yellow. We can't live unless we have access to these tools, and our masters, the capitalists, see to it that we are separated from what we make by using these things, except so much as is necessary to keep us alive that we may be able to make more—for them. This little bit is called wages. They wouldn't give us even that if they thought that we could live without it. In the good old days the chattel-slave would be fastened with a chain if they thougt that he might escape. Today no chain is neccesary to bind us to the tools. We are as free as air. Of course. We are free to starve. And that chain of the-fear-of-starvation binds us to the tools owned by the capitalist as firmly as any iron chain ever did. And this system doesn't care whether the slaves who are bound in this new way are white or black. To the capitalist system all workers are equal—in so far as they have a stomach.

Now the one great fact for the Negro in America today is Race Prejudice. The great labor problem with which all working-people are faced is made harder for black working.-people by the addition of a race problem. I want to show you how one grows out of the other and how, at bottom, they are both the same thing. In other words, I want you to see the economic reason for race-prejudice.

In the first place, do you know that the most rabid, Negro-hating, southern aristocrat has not the slightest objection to sleeping in the same house with a Negro—if that Negro sleeps there as his servant? He doesn't care if his food is prepared by a Negro cook and handled by a Negro waiter before it gets to him; he will eat it. But if a Negro comes into the same public restaurant to buy and eat food, then, Oh my!, he gets all het up about it. But why? What's the difference? I will tell you. The aristocrat wants the black man to feel that he is on a lower level. When he is on that level he is "in his place". When he is "in his place" he is liked. But he must not be allowed to do anything to make him forget that he is on this lower level; he must be kept " in his place", which means the place which the aristocrat wants him to keep. You see, the black man carries the memory of slavery with him. Everybody knows that the slaves were the exploited working-class of the South. That put them in a class by themselves, down at the bottom, downtrodden, despised, "inferior."

Do you begin to see now that Race Prejudice is only another name for Caste Prejudice?

WHAT SOCIALISM MEANS TO US

If our people had never been slaves; had never been exploited workrs, and so, at the bottom of the ladder, there would be no prejudice against them now. In every case where there has been a downtrodden class of workers at the bottom, that class has been despised by the class that lived by their labor. Do you doubt it? Then look at the facts. If you had picked up a daily paper in New York in 1848 you would have found at the end of many an advertisement for butler, coachman, lady's maid, clerk or book-keeper these words: "No Irish need apply." There was a race-prejudice aginst the Irish then, because most of the manual unskilled laborers were Irish. They were at the bottom, exploited and despised. But they have changed things since. Beginning in the seventies when Jewish laborers began to come here from Russia, Austria and Germany, and lasting even to our own day, there has been race-prejudice against the Jews. And today when the Italian has taken the place which the Irish laborer vacated—at the bottoh—he, too, comes in for his share of this prejudice. In every one of these cases it was the condition of the people—at the bottom as despised, exploited, wage-slaves— that was responsible for the race-prejudice. And it is just so in the black man's case, with this difference: that his color marks what he once was, and even though he should wear a dress suit every evening and own an automobile or a farm he can always be picked out and reminded.

Now, under the present system, exploiting the wage-slave is respectable. I have already shown you that wherever the worker is exploited he is despised. So you will see that despising the wage-slave is quite fashionable. You may recall the name of the great capitalist who said, "the public be damned." He was only a little more outspoken than the rest of his class. As long as the present system continues, the workers will be despised; as long as the workers are despised, the black men will be despised, robbed and murdered, because they are least able to defend themselves. Now ask yourself whether you haven't a very special interest in changing the present system.

Of course, you will ask: "But haven't white working people race-prejudice too?" Sure, they have. Do you konw why? It pays the capitalist to keep the workers divided. So he creates and keeps alive these prejudices. He gets them to believe that their interests are different. Then he uses one half of them to club the other half with. In Russia when the workingmen demand reform the capitalists sic them on the Jews. In America they sic them on the Negroes. That makes them forget their own condition: as long as they can be made to look down upon another class. "But, then", you will say, " the average wage-slave must be a chump." Sure, he is. That's what the capitalist counts on. And Socialism is working to educate the workers to see this and to unite them in doing away with the present system.

Socialism stands for the emancipation of the wage-slaves. Are you a wage-slave? Do you want to be emancipated? Then join hands with the Socialists. Hear what they have to say. Read some of their literature. Get a Socialist leaflet, a pamphlet, or, better still, a book. You will be convinced of two things: that Socialism is right, and that it is inevitable. It is right because any order of things in which those who work have least while those who work them have most, is wrong. It is inevitable because a system under which the wealth produced by the labor of human hands amounts to more than two hundred and twenty billions a year while many millions live on the verge of starvation, is bound to break down. Therefore, if you wish to join with the other class—conscious, intelligent wage-earners—in putting an end to such a system; if you want to better living conditions for black men as well as for white men; to make this woful world of ours a little better for your children and your children's children, study Socialism—and think and work your way out.

Twelve years ago Mark Hanna, the Big Boss of the Republican Party, made a statement which you would do well to consider. After he had made McKinley president, he noticed something that you may not have noticed yourself. He saw that there was no essential difference between the Republican party and the Democratic party. He knew that the same big Wall Street companies supplied the campaign funds for each of them. He knew that the same money power was buying out the men whom you elected, whether you elected

Republicans or Democrats. He saw that very soon you and I and the rest of us, black as well as white, would come to see it too. And he opened his mouth and spake these words: "The next great political battle in this country will be fought, not between the Republican and the Democratic parties, but between the Republican party and Socialism." I will tell you later what that implies. But just now, what I should like you to see is this: that Senator Hanna realized that Socialism was a serious issue. He couldn't afford to pooh-pooh it. Neither can any sensible person. The Socialist party is the third in point of numbers. It is important. What do you know of this party? Have you ever read its platform? Read it once, just for the sake of fair play—just to show that you are not afraid to give it a hearing—and you will realize why Mark Hanna paid it such a tribute of respect.

Don't be a baby any longer and listen to the stale lies which other people tell you about Socialism. Read the Socialist platform and you will understand why some politicians have to tell lies about it just the same as they have to tell lies about you. They lie about it because they don't want you to know what it really is, just as they lie about you because they don't want people to know what you really are. Every year they feed you with the same soft mush around election time to help them to ride into power on your votes; then after election they give you Brownsville and lynching bees. Do you wonder that General Clarkson, a grandson of the

great abolitionist, when he gave up his job as col-
lector of the Port of New York, said that he was
sick of the way in which the Republican party was
selling you out? The Republican party is always
engaged in selling you out—or in selling out the
working people of this country. Do you doubt it?
Then ask yourselves why is it that a Republican
Congress has never said a word or done anything
about the disfranchisement of nearly three million
Negro voters in the South? Read the Fourteenth
and Fifteenth Amendments to the U. S. Constitution and you will see that the Republican party has
always had the power to stop it. But just now I
want to get you interested in the one party that
strikes at the very root of your trouble and that
of every workingman in the country—white and
black alike. I want you to see what is the attitude
of the Socialist Party toward the American Negro.
And for that reason I am introducing to you
the f o l l o w i n g declarations of the attitude
made by Eugene V. Debs, the Socialist candidate
for President, and by other members of the party.
Compare its straight-forward, uncompromising ut-
terances with what the other two parties have said
and done; then look yourself in the face and say
whether it is worth you while to sell your birth-
right and your future freedom—yes, and that of
your children and your children's children—for a
mess of political pottage.

THE NEGRO AND THE NEWSPAPERS

It is not an easy task to plead in the courts of the oppressor against oppression and wrong. It is not easy to get the judgement of the white men of the world against the white man's injustice to the black. But nevertheless the attempt must be made and made again until the seared conscience of the civilized world's hall throbs with righteous indignation at such outrage. "To sin by silence when we should protest makes cowards out of men. The human race has climbed on protest. Had no voice been raised against injustice, ignorance and lust, the Inquisition yet would serve the law and guillotines decide our least disputes. The few who dare must speak and speak again to right the wrongs of many."

The urgent need of speaking out is shown by the following communication from Mr. J. Ellis Barker of London in an interview given to a correspondent of **The New York Age** and published in that paper on December 29th 1910.

"We people in Europe," says Mr. Barker, "do not understand the race problem, and we do not know the colored people, for the simple reason that there are not any colored people in Europe. In London, where I live, there are only a few hundred colored students whom one does not meet. Before I came to the United States my prejudice against the colored people was as great as that of any Southern planter. My prejudice against your race, as I believe the prejudice of most white people, was due rather to ignorance than to ill-will. I had been told in the books and papers published in Europe that the colored people were a race of barbarians

59

THE NEGRO AND THE NEWSPAPERS

and savages. I had been told that the colored people were a worthless set of people, dressed in rags, working a day or two during the week, and loafing during the rest of the time. I was told that the colored people were idle, diseased and vicious. So I imagined that all of them lived in slums and alleys and that the aristocracy of the race consisted of the waiters and railway porters.

I had been told that the colored people only played at science; that their doctors and lawyers were charlatems. I had been told that the people of a mixed race were even worse than pure Negroes; that the mulattoes had lost the primitive virtues of the Negroes and had acquired all of the vices of the whites. A chance encounter with a cultured man of color induced me to look into the race problem and I was perfectly amazed when I discovered how greatly the colored people have been libelled and traduced. I have spent a considerable amount of time with colored people and have met many who are highly cultivated. I have found that among your race you have excellent lawyers, and some of the foremost physicians and surgeons. I have been over a large number of your elementary and higher grade schools and colleges and over Howard University, and I have admired the earnest and resolute determination with which your children try to improve their minds and to raise themselves. In your night schools I have found old men and women, former slaves, who are anxious to learn writing and reading. I have been to the homes of many colored people and I have found them cosy, comfortable, elegant, and peopled by happy and harmonious families. I have come to the conclusion that the race is oppressed and persecuted and very largely because it is not 'known."

But it is not in Europe alone that these baneful effects of calumny appear. Here in America, and even in the south where the bulk of the Negroes live in the midst of a people who resentfully declare that they should be left to deal with the Negro because they alone know him—even there the notion of the Negro, fostered by the press and other agencies of public opinion is as wide of the truth as it can be. To illustrate:

In the March number of Van Norden's Magazine in 1907 there appeared a symposium on The Negro Question. It was composed of expressions of opinion from twelve intelligent southerners, and was followed by an article by Mr. Booker T. Washington. The humor of the think lay in this, that these men were Southern college presidents and heads of banks, had lived all their lives among Negroes, and were, by their own words, proved to be either woefully or willfully ignorant of what the Negro had done and was doing. The mordant irony of fate decreed that Mr. Washington should be the one to present the facts that changed their seeming sapience to Falstaffian farce. The president of Randolph-Macon Woman's College, Va. set forth that the Negro will not work regularly, that he needs but three dollars a week and, therefore, works but three days to get it and "quits work to

THE NEGRO AND THE NEWSPAPARS

spend it." The president of Howard College, Alabama declared that, "My deliberate opinion is that the days of the Negro as a fair, honest laborer are numbered, and are few at that. He is becoming daily more shiftless, more unreliable, more restless, less inclined to work steadily." The president of the University of South Carolina and the president of the North Carolina College of Agriculture and Mechanic Arts re-echoed the same doleful dictum while the president of the First National Bank of Birmingham, Ala. and the president of the Bank of Lexington, N. C. declared that it was a mistake to grant the rights of citizenship to the Negro and that education was a curse to him. The president of Guilford College repeated the "lazy, shiftless" argument while the president of Randolph-Macon College, Va. said, "Reduce their wages so that they shall have to work all the time to make a living and they will become better workmen or disappear in the struggle for existence," repeating in substance, the argument of his brother-president of the Woman's college.

   Mr. Washington's article did not show any sign that it had been written as a reply of any sort. But it did show among other things, that the census of 1900 proved that the Negro people **owned** in the very states of these college presidents, "23,-383 square miles of territory, an area nearly as large as that of Holland and Belgium combined"; that this represented only a quarter of the farms worked by them; that, "after a searching investigation, I have not been able to find that a single graduate of Tuskegee, Hampton or any of the Ne-

62

gro colleges can now be found in the prisons of the South;" that in a single county of Virginia-Gloucester Co.—Negroes were paying taxes on land valued at 88 million dollars and on buildings assessed at 80 millions, and all this on the soil wheie they had been slaves forty years before.

Is not this eloquent of the value of American opinion on the American Negro as given in the American press? And the question suggested is, whether such statements are published in ignorance or ill-will? In either case it is equally damnatory.

In December 1907 Professor R. R. Wright, Jr., an eminent Negro sociologist, published in McGirt's Magazine an article on "The Newspapers and the Negro", showing how the Negro is being "done" by headlines and other newspaper devices. The Horizon, at that time the most brilliant Negro prodical, dealt with the subject in its issue for April 1908. Under the caption, "The Color Line in the Press Dispatches", it quoted approvingly these words of a Socialist paper—The Appeal to Reason —"The hand that fakes the Associated Press is the hand that rules the world." European readers who are acquainted with the occasional diversions of Reuter's Hong Kong and Shanghai correspondents will appreciate the point.

The Horizon was constrained to refer to the matter again in its August issue. In both instances specific cases were cited and proof given. Since that time the need of some formal protest has been growing in the minds of all those thinking Negroes who are not compelled to "crook the pregnant hinges of the Knee"; and it has grown largely because the practices complained of have grown to alarming proportions.

The newspapers of this country have many crimes to answer for. They feature our criminals in bold head lines: our substantial men when noticed at all are relegated to the agate type division. Their methods, whether they obtain through set purpose or through carelessness, constantly appeal to the putrid passion of race hatred. They cause rapine to break loose by nurturing rancor. They help create untold sorrow. They are week-kneed and apologizing when the hour is bloody.

But how can such a protest be effectively put? Though Truth come hot on the heels of Falsehood it could not quite undo its devil's work. And the detractors of the weak and helpless are well aware of this.

But Truth in the Negro's case is not even unleashed. Truth, in fact, is chained up and well guarded, and it is this terrible task of setting Truth free that the Negro must essay in the very teeth of the American press. It is not an easy task to voice an adequate protest, for it needs the widest publicity. And since prejudice will oppose, it needs prestige also. Any such effort must feel itself feeble, and yet it must be made.

www.ingramcontent.com/pod-product-compliance
Lightning Source LLC
Chambersburg PA
CBHW051504270326
41933CB00021BA/3467